BIOGRAPHIC
MARLEY

BIOGRAPHIC
MARLEY

LIZ FLAVELL

**ILLUSTRATED BY
MATT CARR**

AMMONITE
PRESS

First published 2019 by
Ammonite Press
an imprint of Guild of Master Craftsman Publications Ltd
Castle Place, 166 High Street, Lewes, East Sussex, BN7 1XU,
United Kingdom
www.ammonitepress.com

Text © Liz Flavell, 2019
Copyright in the Work © GMC Publications Ltd, 2019

ISBN 978 1 78145 372 8

Publisher: Jason Hook
Concept Design: Matt Carr
Design & Illustration: Matt Carr & Robin Shields
Editor: Jamie Pumfrey

Colour reproduction by GMC Reprographics
Printed and bound in Turkey

CONTENTS

ICONOGRAPHIC 06

INTRODUCTION 08

01: LIFE 11

02: WORLD 33

03: WORK 55

04: LEGACY 75

BIOGRAPHIES 92

INDEX 94

ICONOGRAPHIC

WHEN WE CAN RECOGNIZE A MUSICIAN BY A SET OF ICONS, WE CAN ALSO RECOGNIZE HOW COMPLETELY THAT ARTIST AND THEIR MUSIC HAVE ENTERED OUR CULTURE AND OUR CONSCIOUSNESS.

INTRODUCTION

The golden age of rock music has more than its share of icons but the first superstar from the developing world – the man that bridged the gap between reggae and rock – is Bob Marley. In 2017, nearly 40 years after his death, his compilation album *Legend* notched up 500 weeks in the US Billboard charts – a feat only surpassed by Pink Floyd with their album *Dark Side of the Moon*. The bestselling double album has found its way into many people's music collections or playlists because it's packed with songs that have universal appeal. And still, more than 35 years after its release, it sells over a quarter of a million copies a year in the US.

But it's not just the greatest hits that people remember, Marley's songs reached far and wide with a message that resonates across the generations. In 'Trench Town Rock' – Marley's anthem to growing up in a ghetto – he found music was the panacea for pain. Later, in 'One Love' he used music to bring people together to 'feel all right' – a far-reaching message to people from all backgrounds and races. Ultimately, Marley chose music as his messenger because it was what he knew, but also because he instinctively understood its power to heal and to unite people.

MARLEY

8

The life of Bob Marley could easily have played out very differently. The mixed-race child of a black mother and white father growing up in the countryside of Jamaica immediately after the Second World War seemed unlikely to be well known outside his native Jamaica. The light-skinned boy running barefoot with the goats or sleeping under the shade of a mango tree probably never dreamed of being a star. And the young man in sharp suits who slept near a dustbin on the poverty-stricken streets of Trench Town didn't seek fame and fortune. However, like many misfits, he sought some kind of belonging through music. And it was this gift for music that eventually brought solace and superstardom.

"HE GREW UP IN THE GHETTO WHERE THERE WAS NO CARING OR SHARING AND EVERYONE IS OUT FOR THEMSELVES. HE RECOGNIZED IT'S NOT JUST A COLOUR THING. HIS MESSAGE WAS TO STAND UP FOR EVERYONE'S RIGHTS, NOT JUST FOR ONE COLOUR. IT WAS A MESSAGE FOR EVERYONE ROUND THE WORLD WHO WAS SUFFERING — IN INDIA, CHINA, RUSSIA, JAPAN."

—Junior Marvin, *The Telegraph*, 2018

Bob Marley and the Wailers broke the international scene in 1973 with *Catch a Fire*, their first album release through Island Records. By 1977, while the band were in exile in England after an assassination attempt on Marley, they were scoring UK top ten hits and selling out concerts in Europe and the US. Marley achieved hero status upon his return to Jamaica in 1978 when he brought the leaders of the opposition parties together on stage at the One Love concert. By 1980, Marley was an international star who could pull crowds to rival bands such as the Rolling Stones, and he was chosen to perform before royal dignitaries at the independence celebrations in Zimbabwe.

"THE GREATNESS OF A MAN IS NOT IN HOW MUCH WEALTH HE ACQUIRES, BUT IN HIS INTEGRITY AND HIS ABILITY TO AFFECT THOSE AROUND HIM POSITIVELY."

—Bob Marley

Sadly the band's success was shortlived, as Marley had little more than a year to live. His fire burned briefly but his legacy lives on. Through 50 icons and infographics we bring the man, his music and his Rastafarian message to life in an original way. What did he eat? Who did he love and what were his favourite guitars? Along the way, we find out about the history of Jamaica and the birth of reggae. It's a journey that reveals the spirit and the enduring legacy of the king of reggae.

MARLEY

10

BOB MARLEY

01
LIFE

"YOU KNOW WHAT THEM CALL ME, HALF CASTE OR WH'EVER. WELL, ME DON'T DIP ON NOBODY'S SIDE, ME DON'T DIP ON THE BLACK MAN'S SIDE NOR THE WHITE MAN'S SIDE, ME DIP ON GOD'S SIDE, THE MAN WHO CREATE ME, WHO CAUSE ME TO COME FROM BLACK AND WHITE, WHO GIVE ME THIS TALENT"

—Bob Marley, *Melody Maker*, 1975

BOB MARLEY

**was born on 6 February 1945
in Nine Mile, Saint Ann Parish, Jamaica**

Nesta Robert Marley (Bob Marley) was born just before sunrise in his grandfather Omeriah's house in the green and rolling parish of Saint Ann in Jamaica. His mother, Cedella, was just 19. His father, Captain Norval Sinclair Marley, was a white man of English descent who was nearly 60 years old. Norval was not present at the birth nor had he been around much since Cedella had become pregnant. The couple had married in June 1944 and the next day Norval had gone back to Kingston.

As Cedella's bump grew, life carried on pretty much as normal – in the day she worked barefoot in the fields and at night there was often laughter and music. Cedella's father Omeriah played the violin and her uncles joined in on banjo and guitar. The arrival of the first grandson, weighing six and a half pounds, was cause for much celebration in Omeriah's household. Norval returned the week following the birth and named his son Nesta in honour of his brother.

WELCOME TO NINE MILE DRIVE CAREFULLY

MARLEY

14

POPULATION IN 1945

1.3m

GAINED INDEPENDENCE FROM UK

1962

JAMAICA

The political leader **Marcus Garvey** was born in Saint Ann's Bay, the capital of Saint Ann, in 1887. ▶

LIFE

15

JAMAICA

As a British colony, many Jamaicans are enlisted to serve in the Second World War. More than 5,000 men leave their homeland to contribute to the war effort. On the day of Bob's birth, war dominates the front cover of Jamaica's national paper, the *Daily Gleaner.*

The Daily Gleaner

ALLIES WIN VICTORY!

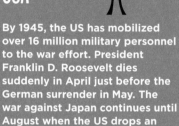

USA

By 1945, the US has mobilized over 16 million military personnel to the war effort. President Franklin D. Roosevelt dies suddenly in April just before the German surrender in May. The war against Japan continues until August when the US drops an atomic bomb on Hiroshima.

UK

On Victory in Europe Day (VE Day) on 8 May the British take to the streets to celebrate the end of the war. With an estimated 383,600 British military fatalities, there is much to be sad about but, after six years of war, victory feels good.

THE WORLD IN 1945

Marley was born seven months before the end of the Second World War. As a British colony, Jamaica sent troops to help with the war effort and there was also an influx of American servicemen as the US established naval bases on the island.

MARLEY

16

SOVIET UNION

The Soviets call it the Great Patriotic War and are jubilant that they have defeated Hitler. In the process an estimated 27 million military and civilian Russians have been sacrificed.

GERMANY

Germany is a nation under attack from Allied forces and on the brink of surrender. During March, the Western Allies cross the river Rhine and in April the Soviets take Berlin. Adolf Hitler commits suicide and the Third Reich is defeated.

FRANCE

The Allies liberate Paris in 1944 and by 1945 the nation is engaged in the war against Germany. The death toll in France is high, with around 1.3 million military deaths and 4.6 million wounded.

ALSO BORN IN 1945

10 JANUARY
ROD STEWART

30 MARCH
ERIC CLAPTON

6 MAY
BOB SEGER

19 MAY
PETE TOWNSHEND

25 JUNE
CARLY SIMON

1 JULY
DEBBIE HARRY

31 AUGUST
VAN MORRISON

12 NOVEMBER
NEIL YOUNG

LIFE

17

BOB'S FAMILY TREE

Bob Marley's father supported his wife and child for a short while before he disappeared from their lives. He died in 1955 when his son was ten. Marley never met his father's family and

FATHER
Norval Marley
(1881–1955)

Nesta Robert Marley
(1945–81)

DAUGHTER
Imani Carole Marley
(1963–)

DAUGHTER
Sharon Marley Prendergast
(1964–)

DAUGHTER
Cedella Marley
(1967–)

SON
David Nesta 'Ziggy' Marley
(1968–)

SON
Stephen Robert Marley
(1972–)

SON
Rohan Anthony Marley
(1972–)

MARLEY

18

was critical of the man he believed abandoned him, but he took his name and made it famous. Marley's own family tree is a complex one, with six daughters and seven sons by nine different mothers.

MOTHERS OF BOB'S CHILDREN

- Rita Marley
- Rita's child adopted by Bob
- Cheryl Murray
- Janet Hunt
- Pat Williams
- Janet Bowen
- Lucy Pounder
- Anita Belnavis
- Cindy Breakspeare
- Yvette Crichton

MOTHER
Cedella Malcolm
(1926–2008)

WIFE
Alpharita Constantia 'Rita' Anderson
(1946–)

DAUGHTER
Karen Marley
(1973–)

SON
Julian Ricardo Marley
(1975–)

SON
Damian Robert Nesta 'Jr. Gong' Marley
(1978–)

SON
Robert Marley
(1972–)

DAUGHTER
Stephanie Marley
(1974–)

SON
Ky-Mani Marley
(1976–)

DAUGHTER
Madeka Jahnesta Marley
(1981–)

LIFE

19

YOUNG MARLEY

1949

Living in the countryside in Nine Mile, Marley runs barefoot in the fields tending to mango trees and looking after his grandfather's goats. At school he is good with numbers. He discovers he can read palms and people come to hear his predictions.

1963

Marley, McIntosh and Livingston and other members of the Wailing Rudeboys (they alternated between this and the Wailers) head to Studio One to record 'Simmer Down' with studio owner Clement 'Sir Coxsone' Dodd. It reaches number one in Jamaica in January 1964.

1962

Dekker takes Marley to meet Leslie Kong at Beverley's Records as well as another new artist called Jimmy Cliff. Marley records his first single co-written with Joe Higgs, called 'Judge Not'. His mother marries again and moves to Delaware, USA. Marley is left homeless and lives on the streets of Trench Town.

STUDIO 1

1965

The Wailers score another hit with 'Rude Boy' and Marley meets his future wife, Rita. He invites her to come for an audition at Studio One and they gradually fall in love.

1966

Marley and Rita marry the day before he moves to Delaware to find work. Marley works shifts at a car plant and a parking lot, and washes dishes – all to save enough money to start a record label. He shows an interest in the religion of Rastafarianism and after six months returns to Jamaica.

1951

When Marley is six, his father suggests that he be schooled in Kingston. His time in the capital doesn't work out as expected, for reasons that are unclear. His father has him adopted and when his mother hears of the arrangement she brings him back to the village.

1955

Marley turns ten, his father dies and his mother moves to Kingston, leaving him behind in the village to be cared for by his grandfather and aunts.

1957

Marley doesn't see his mother for two years, until he gets a message to come and live with her in Trench Town, an infamous slum in Kingston, in a flat in Second Street. Football, fighting and new friends like Bunny Livingston help him to survive in the concrete jungle.

1961

Marley, McIntosh and Livingston rehearse together and the latter teaches Marley to play the guitar. Marley meets singer Desmond Dekker at work.

1960

American artists such as Fats Domino, Ray Charles and Brook Benton fill the airwaves. Bunny fashions a guitar from electrical wire, a sardine can and bamboo. Bob meets Peter McIntosh and, having left school, gets a job in a welding yard.

1968

Marley and Rita have their first son, David 'Ziggy' Marley, and move back to Marley's childhood home in Nine Mile. His record label fails.

1969

Money is tight and Marley goes to the US for work but he returns to Jamaica to be with his family and pursue music. He heads to the recording studio with McIntosh and Livingston and producer Lee 'Scatch' Perry. Perry's studio band, the Upsetters, add rhythm to the Wailers' songs.

CHANGING FACE

Marley's look was clearly defined by his mane of dreadlocks but, if you investigate the clothes instead, another story unfolds. Ironically, in the early days, when he didn't even have a bed of his own, he was well-dressed, wearing the suits that set him apart as a rude boy. Fame and money didn't change the man nor did it make him fill his wardrobe with expensive gear, believing that 'clothes do not maketh the man'.

Marley wore Adidas long before the label became fashionable. For him it was all about comfort and a deep love of football. Curiously, the brand also reminded him of Addis Ababa, the capital of Ethiopia.

RUDE BOY

Money was tight in Trench Town but a decent suit could see you through most things, including church and dancing. Marley wore his black show suit for his wedding to Rita. Sir Coxsone, his producer, bought him a new pair of shoes for the day. Sharp suits and bad-boy swagger were the basis of the classic rude boy look.

SHOWTIME

Sometimes Sir Coxsone would dig deep in his pockets to buy the band some decent stage clothes. At a gig in 1965, at the Glass Bucket in Kingston, Bob Marley and the Wailing Rude-Boy Wailers (as they were billed) wore gold lamé Beatle-style jackets with polka dot shirts. Sharply-pointed black boots were a must.

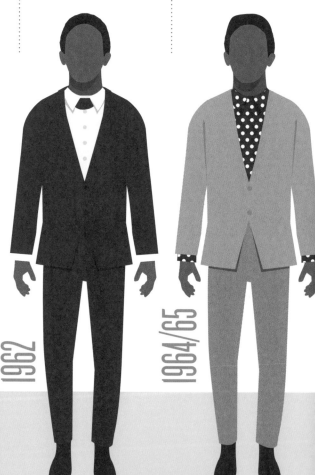

1962

1964/65

MISMATCHED

By 1970 Marley and the band had a few hits in Jamaica but had yet to make any serious money. Clothes were not a high priority and so they began making mismatched clothes look effortlessly cool. A limited wardrobe of denim overalls, waistcoats, hats and patchwork shirts were given a Marley make-over.

DENIM

Bob Marley and the Wailers appeared on the BBC's music show *The Old Grey Whistle Test* in 1973. They performed one of their most famous takes of 'Stir It Up'. Meanwhile, Marley was stirring up the rules of fashion with his double denim look.

RASTAMAN

Marley never overdid the Rastafarian colours, adopted from the Ethiopian flag, of red, green and gold. He wore dazzling bomber jackets and beanies but he always knew to pair them with denim. The same rule applied if he was wearing patterned sweaters or sleeveless jumpers.

1970

1973

1978

LIFE

23

INTERNATIONAL FAME

As a young man with the Wailers, Bob Marley played countless gigs in Kingston. Some time in 1971 the unknown Marley went to New York to record, and later that year he spent time in Sweden with Johnny Nash recording a soundtrack to the film *Want So Much to Believe*. In 1972, he joined Nash on stage for his debut appearance in the UK. The breakthrough year for Bob Marley and the Wailers would ultimately be 1973 with an appearance on the BBC's *The Old Grey Whistle Test* bringing the band to the attention of a fraternity of rock fans in the UK. The band went on to perform over 300 concerts.

UK SOLO DEBUT

COLEMAN CLUB

27 APRIL
1973

• NOTTINGHAM •

COACH HOUSE CLUB

★ 29 MAY 1973
Southampton, UK ★

50–60
ATTENDEES

ADMIT ONE
MATRIX CLUB
30 OCTOBER 1973
SAN FRANCISCO

J. Geils Band, Slade, Boz Scaggs and Faye Dunaway are attendees

UPSTAIRS AT MAX'S KANSAS CITY, NEW YORK

BRUCE SPRINGSTEEN

SPECIAL GUESTS
THE WAILERS

18 July 1973

THE LYCEUM
LONDON
17–18 1975
JULY

Recorded *LIVE!*

2,100
ATTENDEES

£1.50
ADMISSION

RAINBOW THEATRE
4 JUNE 1977
£3 LONDON

MADISON SQUARE GARDEN, NEW YORK
17 JUNE 1978

STADIO SAN SIRO
27 JUNE 1980
MILAN, ITALY

2,802
CAPACITY

4
NIGHTS SOLD OUT

20,000
CAPACITY

$9/10
ADMISSION

120,000
ATTENDEES

MARLEY

24

300+

CONCERTS PLAYED BY MARLEY

ASSASSINATION ATTEMPT!

CRIM

1976

DATE:
3 December

TIME:
Around 8.50 pm

LOCATION:
56 Hope Road, Kingston

KINGSTON POLICE DEPT.

On 5 December 1976, Marley was due to headline a free concert called Smile Jamaica at National Heroes Park, Kingston. At the time Jamaica was rife with conflict. Gun crime and murder were everyday news on the streets of Kingston and Marley had received at least one mumbled warning over the telephone. He had been advised not to go ahead with the concert and had a premonition in a dream. Despite this, Marley pushed on. But, just two days prior to the concert, as the band were rehearsing, masked men raided his villa.

KINGSTON

OFFICIAL

EAST KINGS ROAD

HOPE ROAD

LADY MUSGRAVE RD

56 HOPE ROAD

MARLEY

26

CENE DO NOT CROSS ///

POLICE REPORT

"SMILE JAMAICA"

The Scene:
Rehearsals for the Smile Jamaica concert began at sunset.
The band were playing 'Jah Live' when the events began.

CRIME SCENE 1

Driveway:
Rita Marley is pulling out of the drive in her car, with her friend Louis Simpson in the back. Another car, not involved in the crime, is also being driven out. As the gates open, two white Datsun cars drive in.

The Crime
Bullets hit Rita's car as she attempts to drive away. One bullet grazes her head and is lodged between her skull and scalp – her thick dreadlocks save her life. Simpson is also injured in the attack.

After 2 minutes: Marley, Rita and manager Don Taylor are rushed to hospital.

10 minutes: the police arrive.

20 minutes: Hope Road is empty except for the police.

4 hours: Marley and his friends go to a 'secret' location – Strawberry Hill, a colonial mansion owned by record producer Chris Blackwell located in the hills above Kingston. They are surrounded by armed police guards.

CRIME SCENE 2

Kitchen:
Marley is peeling a grapefruit, band member Donald Kinsey is getting a drink and manager Don Taylor is walking towards Marley.

The Crime
Seven masked men with sub-machine guns jump out of two white cars. Two move to the front door. The rest run round the back and shoot at the windows. Gunmen enter the kitchen and begin shooting. They aim for Marley's heart but hit Taylor instead. One bullet grazes Marley's chest and another hits him in the elbow. Taylor takes five bullets in the waist and side and appears to be badly injured. Kinsey escapes unscathed.

DON TAYLOR

SUSPECTS WERE ARRESTED OR CHARGED

LIFE

27

KICKABOUT!

Marley regularly played football in London parks such as Battersea and Kennington. Reggae artist Eddie Grant often joined him.

LONDON CALLING!

PUNK!

A strong link between punk and reggae was forged when Marley recorded 'Punky Reggae Party' on which he referenced The Clash, The Damned and The Jam. On 1 January 1977, The Clash headlined the opening night of the Roxy Club.

ICONIC RECORDS

Marley's time in London was musically productive. He and the band jammed regularly and wrote new material. Both *Exodus* and *Kaya* were recorded at Island Studios in Notting Hill.

1977

After the assassination attempt in Jamaica in December 1976, Marley spent a month in the Bahamas at Chris Blackwell's studio, before heading to London (which he had first visited in 1972). He took over a luxury flat in Chelsea, sharing it with Rita and the rest of the band. His time in London allowed him to be more creative and he recorded two albums, now widely accepted as some of his finest work. After two years in self-imposed exile, he returned to Jamaica.

MUSIC VIDEO

Marley's video for 'Is this Love' was shot at the Keskidee Centre in North London in 1977. A young Naomi Campbell can be seen dancing in the background.

THE RING

Marley was given an audience with the Ethiopian Crown Prince Asfa Wossen who was living in exile in London. After the two hour meeting, Wossen gave Marley a ring that he said had belonged to his father, Haile Selassie. Marley cherished the ring as Selassie was regarded as God incarnate by Rastafarians.

LIFE

29

AFRICA UNITE!

Marley visited Africa for the first time in 1978. It was a big moment for him – as a Rastafarian he viewed it as a pilgrimage to 'Our Father's Land'. To understand what Africa meant to Marley you need do no more than listen to 'Africa Unite' or the impassioned cry of solidarity in 'Zimbabwe'. He believed Africa was his rightful homeland and dreamed of living there. To this day, Marley is viewed as a hero in Africa and his music inspires younger generations to find their own voice and to 'get up, stand up for their rights'.

1978

ADDIS ABABA

Marley stays in Addis Ababa for four days. He visits many historic sites and attends a rally supporting the liberation movement in Rhodesia, which ultimately inspires him to write 'Zimbabwe'.

LIBREVILLE

Marley's first concert in Africa is at Libreville, the capital of Gabon. The event is part of the birthday celebrations for the president, Omar Bongo. Marley's manager at the time, Don Taylor, is fired after Marley discovers him pocketing $20,000 of the fee for the Gabon gig.

SURVIVAL

The artwork for Marley's ninth album *Survival* features a montage of flags from independent African nations.

MARLEY

30

ZIMBABWE INDEPENDENCE

Rhodesia became the independent country of Zimbabwe and Marley was invited to perform at the ceremony to be attended by President Robert Mugabe, Prince Charles and Indian Prime Minister Indira Gandhi.

APRIL 18 1980

35,000 Watt PA system

A charted Boeing 707 brought in to carry **21** tons of equipment

$250,000

Marley forfeited his fee so the gig could be free

10 minutes into the warm-up gig police used tear gas on the crowd. Marley left the stage but came back on and as an act of defiance played 20 minutes longer than scheduled.

2 gigs played by Bob Marley and the Wailers. One for the main ceremony and one as a warm-up show.

40,000 people in the audience

LIFE

31

THE FINAL GOODBYES

1980 was a busy and productive year for Marley. He was touring and making music until he collapsed in New York. In the months that followed, those close to him saw the life draining out of him, but for those that saw his final performances or heard his last songs, he was full of life.

FINAL ALBUM

Between January and April 1980, Bob and the Wailers were at Tuff Gong Studios in Jamaica recording what would be their final album, *Uprising*. The closing track, 'Redemption Song', was a different approach to reggae, with just Marley and his acoustic guitar.

FINAL EUROPEAN TOUR

In May 1980, Marley's final European tour kicked off in Zurich, Switzerland.

1980

33 CONCERTS

Marley's last concert in Europe was in Stafford, England on 13 July 1980

120,000
audience at Milan's San Siro Stadium on 27 June 1980

FINAL US TOUR

The US tour began on 16 September 1980 in Boston, followed by Rhode Island and two nights in New York. On 21 September, as he was jogging in New York's Central Park, Marley collapsed. In Pittsburgh, two days later, he gave his final live performance. The last song he performed was 'Get Up, Stand Up'. The rest of the tour was cancelled due to 'exhaustion'.

4
CONCERTS

Ticket stub from Marley's last concert in Pittsburgh

WHAT WAS WRONG MARLEY?

After his collapse, Marley was diagnosed with a brain tumour and was given just three weeks to live. After the tour was cancelled, further tests revealed the cancer had spread to his stomach and lungs.

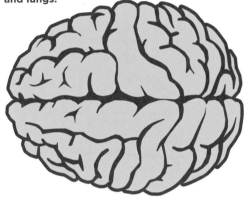

FINAL TREATMENT

Marley travelled to the Sunshine House Cancer Clinic in Rottach-Egern, a small town in the Bavarian foothills of Germany, in late 1980.

The two-hour daily treatment consisted of:

Vaccines injected straight into the stomach.	Diet of whole grains, fibre, herb tea and selected minerals and vitamins.

20%
CHANCE OF SUCCESS

By May it was clear the treatment was not working. Marley weighed less than 85 lbs (38.5 kg).

LIFE

33

DEATH OF AN ICON

On 11 May 1981, just after 11.30am, Bob Marley passed away in the Cedars of Lebanon Hospital in Miami. He had left Germany just 40 hours before to return home. He never made it back to Jamaica.

He was

36

years old

The state funeral took place on

21 MAY 1981

The day before his funeral, his open coffin was viewed by around

100,000

people

Approximately

6,000

people came to the funeral service at the National Arena

The funeral cortége travelled 50 miles from Kingston to Bob Marley's final resting place at his birthplace in Nine Mile, Mount Zion.

MOUNT ZION

JAMAICA

2

flags were draped over Marley's coffin – the green, gold and black flag of Jamaica and the red, green and gold flag of Ethiopia.

A twig of marijuana, his red Gibson guitar, a football, a Bible opened at Psalm 23 and the ring from Haile Selassie ...

... were placed inside his coffin.

"MONEY CAN'T BUY LIFE."

—Bob Marley, final words to his son Ziggy

BOB MARLEY

02
WORLD

"THE MUSIC IS THE BIGGEST GUN, BECAUSE IT SAVE. IT NUH KILL, RIGHT?

THE OTHER GUN LICK OFF YA HEAD!"

—Bob Marley,
Bob Marley by
Steven Davis, 1978

JAMAICA: A HISTORY

Around 2,500 years ago, the Arawak people from South America crossed the Caribbean Sea and landed on Jamaica. They found the sunny island was perfect for growing an abundance of fruit and vegetables such as sweet potatoes, and in the hills they could cultivate tobacco. They called it 'Xaymaca', meaning 'land of wood and water'. The history of this lush Caribbean island is filled with suffering, but its people remember stories of rebellion and the songs of freedom. Today there is a richness in the culture expressed through its music and laid-back living.

MONTEGO BAY

FALMOUTH

JAMA

SAVANNA-LA-MAR

BLACK RIVER

MANDEVILLE

SLAVERY

Slaves were brought from Africa to work the fields. Major uprisings included the Easter Rebellion of 1760 and the Christmas Rebellion of 1831 when plantation owners were killed. Abolition of slavery took place in 1808 with full freedom in 1838.

SPANISH TOWN

Christopher Columbus suggested he discovered Jamaica in 1494. In fact he landed there, murdered local Arawaks and claimed land for the Spanish. In 1509, the colonial administrator Juan de Esquivel arrived and again captured, tortured and murdered many of the Arawaks. The Spanish finally settled around the Saint Ann's Bay area and made their capital Spanish Town.

MARLEY

38

SUGAR CANE

Sugar took over from tobacco as the cash crop of choice when the English colonized the island.

Number of sugar plantations

1673 — 57

1739 — 430

PORT ROYAL

In 1655, the English took control of the island and the Spanish retreated to Cuba. A whole new era began as buccaneers landed their ill-gotten gains and built a town called Port Royal. Meanwhile, the British developed tobacco, coffee, cotton and sugar-cane plantations.

SAINT ANN'S BAY

PORT MARIA

PORT ANTONIO

CA

SPANISH TOWN

KINGSTON

MAY PEN

PORT ROYAL

MORANT BAY

KINGSTON

By 1863, sugar was no longer king – the plantation owners turned to coffee and bananas and paid the freed slaves to work their fields. It took time for the economy to recover from the decline of sugar and the end of slavery but eventually new roads and railways were built. In 1872, Kingston was made the new capital city.

INDEPENDENCE

By the mid-20th century, tourism and bauxite mining were transforming the country's fortunes. In 1958, leader Norman Manley called a referendum in which the people of Jamaica voted for a move towards independence. On 6 August 1962, Jamaica was granted independence from the British.

WORLD

FUNKY KINGSTON

Reggae band Toots and the Maytals called the capital of Jamaica 'Funky Kingston'. From the age of 12, Marley grew up in Trench Town in the St Andrew parish of the city. Named after the sewer over which it was built, it had begun as a shanty town before the government built housing there and called it a 'government yard'. It is the birthplace of rocksteady, ska and reggae and also earned the name 'the Hollywood of Jamaica'. Marley immortalized the hot and dusty streets that were an intrinsic part of his youth in 'Trench Town Rock' and 'No Woman, No Cry'.

STUDIO ONE
13 Brentford Road

The 'Motown' of Jamaica is often credited as the heart and soul of reggae. It was opened in 1963 by Coxsone Dodd. The Wailing Rudeboys dropped by for an audition in August 1963 and cut a few early discs here. An enormous rival to Treasure Isle, Studio One played host to the Heptones, Ken Boothe and a host of other reggae stars.

FEDERAL RECORDS
Marcus Garvey Drive

Bob Marley and the Wailers used Ken Khouri's facilities until they launched their own label Tuff Gong in 1970.

RANDY'S
17 North Parade

Vincent 'Randy' Chin, a Jamaican of Chinese descent, opened his recording studio above his ice-cream parlour and record shop in 1962. Lee Perry was a regular and Marley recorded part of *Catch a Fire* here.

MARLEY'S TEENAGE HOME
19 Second Street

The government yard in Trench Town was built after the hurricane of 1951. Marley moved here in 1957 to live with his mother.

MARLEY

40

DYNAMIC SOUND STUDIOS
15 Bell Road

Reckoned by some to be the oldest studio in Kingston, this is often referred to as the birthplace of ska. Toots and the Maytals recorded 'Funky Kingston' here.

BLACK ARK
Washington Gardens

Reggae superstar and music producer Lee 'Scratch' Perry opened his studio in his own backyard in 1973. Adventurous and innovative, he worked with Bob Marley and the Wailers, the Congos, Pablo Moses, Junior Delgado and Augustus Pablo. The studio burned down in 1980, possibly on purpose.

TREASURE ISLE
33 Bond Street

Owner Duke Reid built a recording studio over his grocery and liquor store in 1964. It was a hotbed for rocksteady and early reggae sounds. Early ska by Prince Buster and Ken Boothe was produced at this hallowed place.

BEVERLEY'S
135 Orange Street

This ice-cream parlour, stationery store and record shop was run by Leslie Kong. He launched the label in 1961 and released Bob Marley's 'Judge Not' and 'One Cup of Coffee'.

MARLEY'S HOME
56 Hope Road, St Andrew

This wooden colonial era house was formerly owned by Chris Blackwell of Island Records. Moving from Trench Town to this area in 1975 was a massive step up for Marley who could now count politicians and celebrities as neighbours. It is now the Bob Marley Museum.

GSTON

Homes

Studios

1962
ROCKING ALL OVER THE WORLD

Marley began writing his own songs in 1961, and in 1962 he released his first single 'Judge Not'. It was an exciting time to be young and part of the music scene in Jamaica. This was the year that Jamaica gained independence from Britain and the first wave of ska music was in full throttle. A few mainstream artists like Sam Cooke and the Drifters from the US were popular but homegrown talent was flooding the airwaves and hitting the streets on great custom-made stacks of speakers called sound systems.

BEST SELLER

'Stranger on the Shore' by Acker Bilk

Elvis has a hit with single 'Good Luck Charm', while his films *Follow that Dream, Kid Galahad* and *Girls! Girls! Girls!* are a success at the box office

R&B

classics include Sam Cooke's 'Twistin' the Night Away', Booker T. & the M.Gs' 'Green Onions' and Ray Charles' 'Unchain My Heart'

UNITED STATES

JAMAICA

Chart-toppers: Jimmy Cliff, Laurel Aitken, David Brown, Girl Satchmo

Jimmy Cliff hits include 'Hurricane Hattie', 'Miss Jamaica' and 'Since Lately'

'Forward March' by Derrick Morgan, which celebrated Jamaican independence, was a dancehall floor-filler

17 UK chart position for The Beatles' 'Love Me Do'

Chart-toppers: Elvis Presley, Cliff Richard, Tornados

BEST SELLER

'I Remember You' by Frank Ifield

UNITED KINGDOM

Chart-toppers: Charles Aznavour, Johnny Hallyday, Petula Clark

Johnny Hallyday is lauded as the 'French Elvis'. His number one hits include 'Retiens la Nuit' and 'L'Idole des Jeunes'

Isabelle Aubret wins the Eurovision Song Contest with 'Un Premier Amour'

FRANCE

"WE COULDN'T AFFORD TO BUY RECORDS SO WE LISTENED TO THE RADIO."

REGGAE ROOTS

Bob Marley is cited as reggae's biggest star, yet he was following in the footsteps of musicians who had employed the distinctive heavy four-beat rhythm to make ska music back in the 1960s. The new beat went through many tweaks and changes before it became the sound we know today – but how did it get there and what were the defining moments of its evolution?

1800s

CALYPSO

An import from Trinidad & Tobago to Jamaica in the 19th century, these rhythmic and harmonic vocals have distinctive African and French influences.

1950s

MENTO

This homegrown folksy music is often mistaken calypso. Expect acoustic guitar, banjos, hand drum and rhumba box with fu real-life or rude lyrics. It heyday was in the 1950s with the advent of recor

1960s

1966

1968

SKA

ROCK STEADY

REGGAE

Upbeat dance music with an emphasis on the off-beat explodes onto the scene in the early 1960s. Influenced by mento, calypso, US jazz and rhythm and blues, ska bands feature bass, drums, guitar, keyboards and plenty of horns.

When rocksteady hits the scene in 1966 the tempo slows down. Characterized by booming backbeat basslines and one-drop drum beat, rocksteady is the stepping stone to reggae. As with its big brother ska, the lyrics are fun and great for skanking.

The tempo slows down again when reggae finds its feet in 1968. The backbeat bassline and one-drop drum hit get louder but the emphasis is still on the offbeat. Thanks to Bob Marley, Toots & the Maytals and others, the lyrics tend to have a more spiritual or political agenda.

WORLD

45

GANJA!

In Jamaica cannabis is commonly called 'ganja', a Hindi word which originated in India from the river Ganges where the cannabis plant grows naturally and in abundance. The plant was introduced to Jamaica between 1850 and 1860, and has become synonymous with the Rastafarian and reggae culture. Marley viewed smoking cannabis as a holy rite and believed it opened up his mind as he furthered his spiritual journey.

Marijuana contains around **480** naturally occurring chemicals. Scientists are still puzzling out what all these chemicals can do but what is certain is that they produce an array of psychoactive, therapeutic and sedative effects. It is hoped that treatments for cancer and neurodegenerative diseases will also be found within the magical, mysterious plant.

CANNABIS PLANT
(Cannabis sativa)

MARLEY NATURAL

Marley Natural is the US cannabis business started by Marley's family in 2016. Customers can buy an array of different cannabis products.

Ganja has been illegal in Jamaica but in 2015 the laws regarding small amounts for personal use have changed

MARLEY

46

"HERB IS THE HEALING OF THE NATION, ALCOHOL IS THE DESTRUCTION."

—Bob Marley

30%

of the plant is Delta-9 tetrahydro-cannabinol (THC or the bit that makes you feel high)

THC

Despite his use of the herb since 1966, Marley was only arrested in Jamaica for possession once, in 1968. The law caught up with him in London in 1977: he appeared at Marylebone Magistrates' Court for possession of cannabis. Marley was fined £50 for possession of two Thai sticks (dried marijuana tied into long sticks).

2 OZ

(56.6g) is now the maximum you're allowed to have in your possession.

WORLD

47

RASTA MAN

Bob Marley became interested in the Rastafari religion and becoming a Rastafarian (Rasta) in the 1960s. By the 1970s he claimed: "Rastafari not a culture, it's a reality". This religious movement started in Jamaica in the 1930s following the succession of Ras Tafari Makonnen (1893–1975), better known as Haile Selassie, to the Ethiopian throne. Jamaican politician and black activist Marcus Garvey (1887–1940) had prophesied in 1927 that a black king would be crowned in Africa, and Rastas came to believe that Selassie was the incarnation of their God, who they called Jah.

HAILE SELASSIE

Rastas call Haile Selassie 'King of Kings and Lord of Lords, Conquering Lion of the Tribe of Judah'

ALCOHOL & CIGARETTES

Tools of Babylon that confuse the mind

ONE LOVE?

Rasta men can have many sexual partners. For women only one man!

RICHNESS IS IN LIF

LIVE A NATURAL LIF

MARLEY

48

ITAL COOKING

'Ital' (or 'vital') food is pure food which is mostly vegetarian (no pork or salt)

GANJA

Opens the mind and purifies the soul

BIBLE

A holy text that has been corrupted: Rastafarians look for the true meaning in 'the book within'

PREACH PEACE

NOT VIOLENCE

ZION

Zion is the City of God, and Africa is Zion. Ethiopia is the promised land of Heaven on Earth. Rastafari are on a quest to discover true black identity.

JAH

Jah (Jehovah) is within every human being: "God is man and man is God"

BABYLON

Babylon is the ultimate evil.

WESTERN SOCIETY
↓
EXILE
↓
SLAVERY
↓
CAPITALISM
↓
COLONIALISM
↓
BABYLON

OT POSSESSIONS

RGET ABOUT THE SYSTEM

WORLD

49

BOB'S LOCKS

1968

Marley's mother Cedella is a Christian and disapproves of his budding locks. He cuts them off despite having adopted the Rastafarian faith.

1972

Marley's hair is growing longer and he wears his hair twisted and styled in an Afro.

1966

In Delaware, Marley's hair starts to get bushier and sometimes he wears it back. After a trim he gathers the clippings, pops them in a paper bag and buries them in the garden to prevent the birds from collecting them to make their nests.

Marley starts to 'knot up' his hair soon after coming home from Delaware. He notices that lots of kids in the ghetto are growing dreads and Rita and Bunny Wailer are already growing theirs too.

1973

On the cover of *Catch a Fire*, Marley's dreadlocks are starting to show.

1977

By now, Marley is sporting shoulder-length dreadlocks. Even though his relationship with Rita has cooled off he always turns to her to care for his dreads. It takes a whole day to massage his head, shampoo, dry and oil the dreadlocks.

1980

Bob's dreadlocks reach way down his back. In concert he shakes his head and sets his mane of dreadlocks flying. Some of the most iconic photos of Bob are taken during his live performances as he makes shapes with his dreads.

1974

The album *Natty Dread* is released – Marley's burgeoning dreads and devotion to Rastafari are loud and clear.

NATTY DREADS

Marley was given the nickname 'Natty Dread'. The word 'natty' is the Jamaican way of saying 'naughty', which is what the British would call rastafarians with dreadlocks – although it could also mean 'natural'. Dreadlocks are symbolic of the Lion of Judah sometimes seen in the middle of the Ethiopian flag. Rastafarians are inspired by the Nazarites in the bible who believed it was wrong to shave or comb hair. Natty dread has since come to mean a spiritual person who is ready to fight for their rights.

WORLD

51

FOOTBALL CRAZY

Marley loved football almost as much as music. As a boy growing up in Trench Town he'd get up early to play his guitar or kick a ball around. Even at the height of his fame he'd still get up at 5am each morning to go running so he stayed in shape for the beloved game. At home at Hope Road, he'd play in the yard each day. On tour he'd schedule matches for every place the band stayed. He talked with Brazilian footballer Paulo Cesar Lima (Caju) about starting a football academy in Jamaica but died before he could realize the dream.

FRUITFUL!

At school, Bob played football with oranges and grapefruits as the ball.

1978

The Kaya Tour was planned around the world cup in Argentina.

ON TOUR...

The Wailers played football everywhere they went. If they couldn't find a pitch then they'd play in Marley's suite. They called this 'Money Ball' because if anyone broke anything they had to pay up. The tour bus TV was always turned on to football. Marley preferred watching with the sound switched off because he didn't enjoy the commentary.

MARLEY
10

BOB'S BIG GAMES

BOB MARLEY & THE WAILERS

**9 MAY 1977
PAVILLON BALTARD
PARIS, FRANCE**

BOB MARLEY AND THE WAILERS V POLYMUSCLES

The day before the Paris concert, Marley and his team played against a team comprised of television and cinema celebrities and journalists. During the match, a rough tackle ended in Marley's toenail being ripped off his right big toe.

**19 MARCH 1980
CHICO BUARQUE PITCH
RIO DE JANEIRO, BRAZIL**

BOB MARLEY (TEAM A) V TEAM B

Marley got to play alongside one of his heroes of football from the Brazilian World Cup 1970 squad, Caju, on Brazilian turf.

**16 JULY 1980
LONDON, ENGLAND**

BOB MARLEY AND THE WAILERS V EDDIE GRANT AND THE SONS OF JAH

An indoor game of football against new reggae star Eddie Grant ended in a woeful 5:2 defeat for Marley and the team.

BAREFOOT BOB

Marley injured his right foot many times. Despite this, he always preferred to play football barefoot.

FAVOURITE PLAYERS

Marley's favourite players were Pele (right), Osvaldo Ardiles and Diego Maradona.

MARLEY'S DIET

Marley had a wholesome, natural diet thanks to his Rastafarian way of life. He avoided pork, shellfish and salt. He dined on 'Ital' (vital) foods which include fresh fruit and vegetables, coconut milk, spices, chillies and herbs. The kitchen at his home in Hope Road was open 24 hours with juices, soups and stews always on the menu. On tour, he had his own chef Tony 'Gilly' Gilbert creating the slap-up Ital feasts Marley and the band demanded after each show.

PEANUT JUICE

Peanut juice was another one of Marley's go-to drinks. Packed with protein with aphrodisiac potential, it's blended with condensed milk and a host of spices.

IRISH MOSS

Ingredients: Seaweed, thickeners such as isinglass, linseed, condensed milk, honey, milk, cinnamon, vanilla and spices.

Marley's favourite drink was the seaweed concoction called Irish Moss. It is said to treat anything from bad breath to diarrhoea, but, best of all, it's supposed to be an aphrodisiac.

FISH TEA

Marley loved heading to the beach to eat food cooked on an open fire, especially snapper, parrot fish and yellowtail fresh from the sea. Fish tea, a spicy fish soup featuring yam, pumpkin, cassava, potatoes and green bananas, is good for the mind and body and was another one of his favourites.

ACKEE AND JOHNNYCAKES

Ackee is a fruit native to Jamaica and it goes well with johnnycakes. These chewy fried dumplings were a treat in Trench Town when Marley was growing up.

BOB MARLEY

03
WORK

"MARLEY'S IMAGES OF EXODUS, RESISTANCE AND PARADISE ON EARTH AREN'T JUST JAMAICAN OR EVEN CONFINED TO UNDERDEVELOPED PARTS OF THE WORLD; THEY CAN SPEAK TO EVERYONE THROUGH THE POWER OF HIS MUSIC AS A MODERN DAY UTOPIAN VISION."

—John Rockwell, *New York Times*, 1978

THE WAILING WAILERS
1965

CATCH A FIRE
1973

SOUL REVOLUTION
1971

STUDIO ALBUMS

Bob Marley and the Wailers recorded 13 studio albums and there were also numerous live recordings that were released in Marley's lifetime and posthumously. However, it is the 'best-of' album *Legend*, released in 1984, that introduced many listeners to Bob Marley. Another great addition to any collection is the box-set *Songs of Freedom*. Released in 1992, this four-CD set contained previously unreleased material as well as Marley's moving last live performance of 'Redemption Song' in Pittsburg in September 1980.

THE BEST OF THE WAILERS
1971

SOUL REBELS
1970

BURNIN'
1973

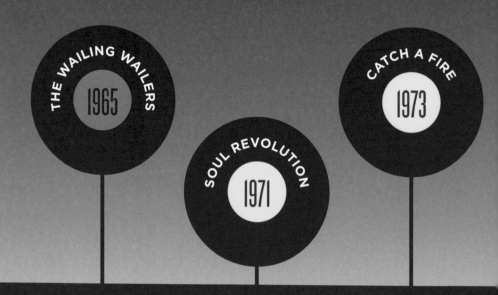
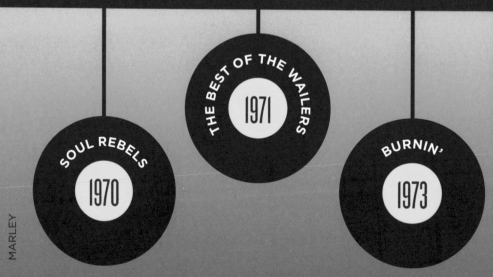

NATTY DREAD 1974

SURVIVAL 1979

EXODUS 1977

CONFRONTATION 1983

"BOB MARLEY WAS NEVER SEEN. HE WAS AN EXPERIENCE WHICH LEFT AN INDELIBLE IMPRINT WITH EACH ENCOUNTER. SUCH A MAN CANNOT BE ERASED FROM THE MIND. HE IS PART OF THE COLLECTIVE CONSCIOUSNESS OF THE NATION."

—Edward Seaga, Prime Minister of Jamaica (1980–89)

KAYA 1978

RASTAMAN VIBRATION 1976

UPRISING 1980

WORK

ANATOMY OF AN ALBUM: CATCH A FIRE

In 1972, Chris Blackwell of Island Records was searching for the band that would break Jamaican music in the international rock market. Jimmy Cliff had been his early gambit but when he left the label, Blackwell began looking for a band with a rebel edge that would appeal to rock fans. When 'Tuff Gong' (Marley's nickname) walked into his office with Bunny Livingston and Peter McIntosh he had an inkling he'd found his man. No contract was needed, Blackwell gave the band £4,000 to begin recording an album with a further £4,000 promised upon completion. Many people told Blackwell he was mad but when the Wailers hit the studio they were hungry for success.

5 CATCH A FIRE STORIES

1. *Catch A Fire* means 'burn in Hell'.
2. Tracks like 'Concrete Jungle' and 'Slave Driver' made a socio-political comment that was new to reggae music.
3. Four of the numbers were remakes of Wailers songs from the 1960s: 'Stir It Up', '400 Years', 'Stop that Train' and 'Concrete Jungle' were updated with synthesizers and even wah wah and bluesy guitar.
4. Romantic songs like 'High Tide or Low Tide' and 'All Day All Night' were deemed too soft for this release, but were included on the 2011 remastered edition.
5. Many of the tracks were longer than the usual reggae norm of a couple of minutes. 'Stir It Up' and 'Midnight Ravers' were over 5 minutes long.

#51 BILLBOARD R&B CHART POSITION

#171 CHART POSITION IN THE USA

RECORDED MAY – OCTOBER 1972

at Dynamic and Harry J Studio, Kingston, Jamaica and Basing Street Studios, London, England

MARLEY

60

ALBUM IN NUMBERS

123

rank on *Rolling Stone* magazine's 500 Greatest Albums of All Time

20,000

number of pressings of the LP that had a Zippo lighter case cover

14,000

copies sold in first year of release

1

shows (out of 19) played on the UK tour before Bunny Wailer left the band

RELEASED
13 APRIL 1973

LENGTH: 37m 51s

SIDE ONE

1. CONCRETE JUNGLE
2. SLAVE DRIVER
3. 400 YEARS
4. STOP THAT TRAIN
5. BABY WE'VE GOT A DATE (ROCK IT BABY)

SIDE TWO

6. STIR IT UP
7. KINKY REGGAE
8. NO MORE TROUBLE
9. MIDNIGHT RAVERS

WORK

61

GUITAR MAN

Marley was an accomplished guitarist, but he didn't possess many guitars – probably between five and seven. As a boy he played a bamboo and goatskin guitar made for him by his cousin Nathan. As a teenager in Trench Town he stayed up late with the light from an oil lamp as he learned chords from a *Teach Yourself Guitar* book. The first proper guitar he 'acquired' was from the Ebenezer Boy's Club – it was tiny and beaten up but did the job until it was accidentally smashed up. Soon after that, the Wailers bought their first full-sized guitar and nicknamed it 'Betsy', the same as Bo Diddley's guitar. They added an electric pick-up and used it with an amp – it was still being played strong in 1967 on some of their early recordings. When Bob owned a few guitars of his own, his philosophy remained simple – love your guitar, make it part of you and keep it around you at all times.

FENDER STRATOCASTER

Rosewood fingerboard finished in a three-tone sunburst. It was stolen from his tour bus in 1971.

1957 GIBSON LES PAUL SPECIAL

Bought in London in 1973, it had already been modified with pearloid block inlays on the neck. More modifications were made by guitar-techno whizz Roger Mayer (of Jimi Hendrix and Pete Townshend fame) in 1979.

MARLEY'S FAVOURITE

YAHAMA SG1000

Given to Marley on tour in Japan in 1979.

MARLEY

62

OVATION ADAMAS

Used for the recording of 'Redemption Song' in 1980.

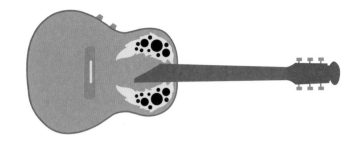

EPIPHONE FT 165 12-STRING

Played during Marley's final gigs of 1980 for a live rendition of 'Redemption Song'.

1972 GUILD 12-STRING

This guitar belonged to Junior Marvin and Marley borrowed it to record 'Is This Love' and 'Time Will Tell' in 1978.

GUILD MADEIRA A-9

Marley decorated it with pictures of Haile Selassie and Africa and the words 'Africa Must Be Free by 1983'.

AMPS

Marley was not much into gear but amplification was important to that deep, rhythmic sound. Fender Silver Face Twin, Marshall and Ampeg amps were all used in his backline.

WORK

63

ANATOMY OF AN ALBUM: EXODUS

Exodus was the first album that Marley recorded outside Jamaica. Following the assassination attempt in December 1976, he moved to London. It was a self-imposed exile and during his time in cold, damp England the band recorded two albums concurrently – *Exodus* and *Kaya*. *Exodus* is certainly an LP with two sides: side one has a strong religious vibe while side two gets more romantic and ends on a message of peace and love for everyone. Ultimately, four of the five tracks on side two went on to become international hits and the album was certified gold and platinum around the world.

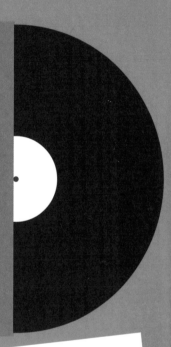

4 EXODUS STORIES

1. 'One Love/ People Get Ready' started out as a simple Wailers ska song in 1965. The remake on *Exodus* has elements of Curtis Mayfield's 'People Get Ready'; Bob admired him, so he is credited on the track.
2. This was the first time the Wailers were let loose in a 24-track studio which added depth and complexity to the sound.
3. Marley fell in love with the then Miss World, Cindy Breakspeare, during the making of *Exodus*. 'Turn Your Lights Down Low' and 'Waiting in Vain' reveal his tender side.
4. Roger Mayer, famed for his work with Jimi Hendrix, visited Marley in Jamaica before he recorded the album. Marley told Mayer he wanted to sound 'international' and that he loved the sound of Jimi Hendrix.

#8 CHART POSITION IN THE UK

#20 CHART POSITION IN THE USA

RECORDED
1976
Harry J Studio, Kingston, Jamaica

JANUARY – APRIL 1977
Island Studios, London, England

MARLEY

64

ALBUM IN NUMBERS

169
rank on *Rolling Stone* magazine's 500 Greatest Albums of All Time

'ALBUM OF THE CENTURY'
As voted by *Time* magazine

5
number of tracks that later featured on Marley's greatest hits album *Legend*

40th Anniversary
In 2017, the album was remastered and released as a three-disc boxset

56
consecutive weeks spent in the UK charts

RELEASED
3 JUNE 1977

LENGTH: 37m 24s

SIDE ONE
1. NATURAL MYSTIC
2. SO MUCH THINGS TO SAY
3. GUILTINESS
4. THE HEATHEN
5. EXODUS

SIDE TWO
6. JAMMING
7. WAITING IN VAIN
8. TURN YOUR LIGHTS DOWN LOW
9. THREE LITTLE BIRDS
10. ONE LOVE/ PEOPLE GET READY

WORK

65

LEGENDARY GIGS

"SMILE JAMAICA"

The idea for the Smile Jamaica festival was inspired by singer Stevie Wonder, who had performed a free concert in Kingston in 1975. Marley wanted to do something similar – as he said: "Jamaica need to smile, because in Jamaica everyone really vex too much." Unfortunately, his event became embroiled in party politics. An election was announced for a few weeks after Smile Jamaica and, though Bob tried to steer clear, he may well have stirred up tensions that led to the assassination attempt a few days prior to the concert.

5 DECEMBER 1978 • NATIONAL HEROES PARK, KINGSTON

Marley said he'd play just 1 song but played **12**

90 minutes on stage

200 people surrounded Marley on stage to protect him against shooters

Just days after being shot, Rita Marley performed at the concert in her hospital gown

80,000 ATTENDEES

"I JUST WANTED TO PLAY FOR THE LOVE OF THE PEOPLE."

—Bob Marley

Marley left his homeland straight after Smile Jamaica. He returned over a year later to a country that was torn apart by politics. Michael Manley had won the election but there was poverty and bloodshed on the streets. Marley funded a festival he named the One Love Peace Festival but which the media called 'Third World Woodstock'. Towards the end of his set, under the light of a full moon, Marley called the rival leaders Michael Manley and Edward Seaga onto the stage to shake hands in a bid for unity. He finished off with 'One Love' and 'Jah Live'.

ONE LOVE

22 APRIL 1978 • THE NATIONAL STADIUM, KINGSTON

TICKET PRICES

$2

Togetherness Section - the cheapest seats were out in the open.

$3

Love Section - these seats were out in the grandstand.

$8

Peace Section - these were VIP tickets.

"I JUST WANT TO SHAKE HANDS AND SHOW THE PEOPLE THAT WE'RE MAKE IT RIGHT"

—Bob Marley

$50,000 **Marley funded the show himself**

32,000 ATTENDEES

ALL PROCEEDS TO LOCAL COMMUNITY PROJECTS

WORK

67

ANATOMY OF AN ALBUM: UPRISING

Uprising was the final album Marley made in his lifetime and possibly his most religious and serious. Though seemingly unaware that the cancer was spreading, his experiences over the previous few years had changed his perspectives on life. Less than a year after its release, Marley passed away. In songs like 'Coming in From the Cold', 'Forever Loving Jah' and 'We and Dem' he finds strength in his faith. On 'Redemption Song', the closing song on the album, Marley swaps his Gibson for an acoustic guitar and sings his ultimate song of freedom. It was only after his passing that people realized he'd penned his own epitaph.

4 UPRISING STORIES

1. The album was recorded at Tuff Gong, the band's new 24-track studio at Marley's home in Hope Road. The equipment was fresh which created a slick different sound.
2. Recording at home offered a whole new experience. Rehearsals started early. Later in the day, Marley played football, showered, ate and then headed back to the studio until five in the morning.
3. Marley had been told by New York DJ Frankie Crocker that to reach young, black American audiences he needed to get funky like James Brown. He took Junior Marvin's riff and ran with it, creating 'Could You Be Loved'.
4. In the verse of 'Could You Be Loved' the backing singers repeat a line from Marley's first single 'Judge Not'.

#1 CHART POSITION IN NEW ZEALAND

#6 CHART POSITION IN THE UK

#3 CHART POSITION IN SWEDEN

#45 CHART POSITION IN THE USA

RECORDED JANUARY – APRIL 1980
Tuff Gong Studios, Kingston, Jamaica

ALBUM IN NUMBERS

0

royalties taken by the band; instead the money was reinvested in the studio

7 million

physical copies sold worldwide

18

hours per day spent in the studio recording the album

11

months between the release of the album and Marley's untimely passing

5

peak position of 'Could You Be Loved' in UK charts

RELEASED
10 JUNE 1980

LENGTH: 35m 53s

SIDE ONE

1. COMING IN FROM THE COLD
2. REAL SITUATION
3. BAD CARD
4. WE AND DEM
5. WORK

SIDE TWO

6. ZION TRAIN
7. PIMPER'S PARADISE
8. COULD YOU BE LOVED
9. FOREVER LOVING JAH
10. REDEMPTION SONG

WORK

69

MARLEY'S BIG BAND

Over the years, Bob Marley was joined by an ever-changing cast of players – musicians and singers who would gather under the name 'the Wailers'. Childhood friends from Trench Town, Bunny Livingston and Peter McIntosh, were along for the ride in the early years. By 1974 they'd left and went on to establish themselves as solo artists Bunny Wailer and Peter Tosh. A new rhythm section with brothers Aston 'Family Man' Barrett and Carlton (Carlie) Barrett joined the line-up. The Barretts and the I Threes, comprising Rita Marley, Marcia Griffiths and Judy Mowatt, were with Marley to the end.

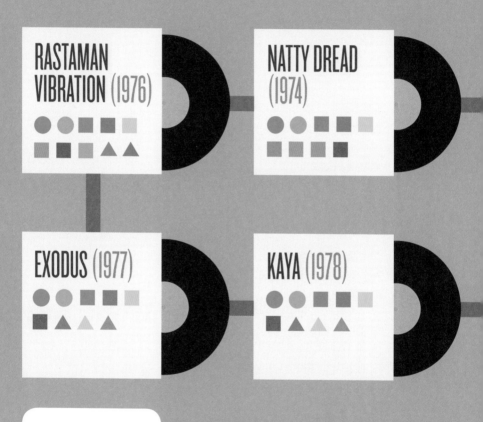

RASTAMAN VIBRATION (1976)

NATTY DREAD (1974)

EXODUS (1977)

KAYA (1978)

PLAYERS

- Bob Marley
- Junior Braithwaite
- Beverley Kelso
- Bunny Livingston
- Rita Marley
- 'Family Man' Barrett
- Marcia Griffiths
- Bernard Harvey
- Don Kinsey
- Tyrone Downie
- Seeco Patterson
- Junior Marvin

MARLEY

70

Over the years Marley's band had...

22 main musicians and singers on his eight albums

JUDGE NOT (1962)

CATCH A FIRE (1973)

THE WAILING WAILERS (1963)

SURVIVAL (1979)

UPRISING (1980)

- ● Peter McIntosh
- ● Cherry Smith
- ● Peter Tosh
- ● Carlton Barrett
- ■ Jean Roussel
- ■ Al Anderson
- ■ Judy Mowatt
- ■ Chinna Smith
- ▲ Earl Lindo
- ▲ Carlton Davis

WORK

71

NO WOMAN NO CRY...

RECORDED LIVE AT THE LYCEUM

In 1975, Bob Marley and the Wailers had international fame at their fingertips and nowhere was this more evident than at their live shows. People of all races and backgrounds came together to experience the Wailers. New additions like the American R&B guitarist Al Anderson brought a bigger sound, while the I Threes' soothing backing vocals added a gospel vibe. At the centre of it all was Marley and when he sang 'No Woman, No Cry' with so much heart, the crowds joined in with every word. The magic was captured on a live recording at the London Lyceum Theatre on 17 July 1975 and it would become their breakthrough international hit.

UK CHART POSITION

1975: 22
1985: 8

'No Woman, No Cry' was always Marley's song but one of his Trench Town pals, Vincent 'Tartar' Ford, was credited as composer. Ford ran a soup kitchen in Kingston and royalties from the record meant he could keep running the place.

The song appeared on the 1974 album *Natty Dread* but, with a simple drum machine and no backing singers, it lacks the passion of the later live versions.

In the song, Georgie's fire is made with logs of wood but in the days when Marley actually sat around in the government yard they burned old rubber tyres through the night.

In quiet moments, Marley liked to write about the world around him. In 'No Woman, No Cry' the hardship of life in Trench Town is laid bare humbly and tenderly. The people and experiences are real but the solace offered is universal.

Years after Marley's death, the rights for 'No Woman, No Cry' and many others he'd credited to friends and band members were challenged unsuccessfully in court. Marley regularly practised this division of royalties so past promoters or managers didn't get a cut.

7:07
MINUTES LONG

MARLEY

72

BOB MARLEY

04
LEGACY

"WE SEE BOB AS A SHEPHERD AND LEADER, AND WE'RE CONFIRMING THAT THE MUSIC GOES ON, NEVER TO DIE. IT'S A MESSAGE OF LOVE AND HOPE... THE HOPE THAT WE WILL GET RID OF WAR AND ILLUSIONS,

AND THAT EVERYTHING WILL COME TO A REALITY IN A ONE-NESS. WE SEE THAT AS SOMETHING THAT CAN SAVE THE WORLD. MUSIC HAS THAT POWER, AND BOB INTENDED TO USE IT AS A WEAPON."

—Rita Marley,
Los Angeles Times, 1984

ONE LOVE

MARLEY IN NUMBERS

A BRIEF HISTORY OF SEVEN KILLINGS

The Man Booker Prize winning novel of 2015 by Marlon James tells the story of the assassination attempt on Marley in 1976

1 WIFE

Rita, who Marley married in 1966

£4,000

The advance paid by Island Records to record the first album

3 LITTLE BIRDS

Marley sometimes called his backing singers, the I Threes, his 'three little birds'

'1 CUP OF COFFEE'

One of four songs Marley recorded in 1962

100,000

The largest audience for Bob Marley and the Wailers in Europe in 1980

1 BEAUTY QUEEN

Relationship with Cindy Breakspeare in 1977

8 MUSICAL CHILDREN

Sharon and Cedella – the Melody Makers; David 'Ziggy' – the Melody Makers and then as a solo artist; Stephen – the Melody Makers and solo; Rohan – as a solo artist and musician; Julian – performing with siblings and solo; Ky-Mani – reggae and dancehall musician; and Damian – reggae musician

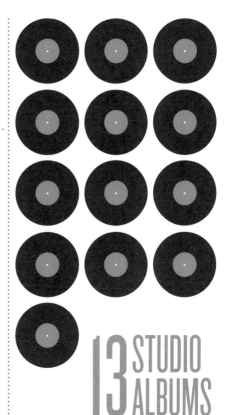

13 STUDIO ALBUMS

"MONEY IS NUMBERS AND NUMBERS NEVER END. IF IT TAKES MONEY TO BE HAPPY, YOUR SEARCH FOR HAPPINESS WILL NEVER END."

—Bob Marley, taken from Ralph Rosell's *The Boy Who Wanted Sex, Fame, Money, Power and Drugs*, 2015

2 CHILDHOOD MUSICIAN FRIENDS

Peter Tosh and Bunny Wailer

LEGACY

77

LEGEND

The album *Legend* is the ultimate introduction to the music of Bob Marley, as it contains 14 of his greatest hits. Released posthumously in 1984, this gatefold LP is the best-selling reggae album of all time, and also holds the distinction of being the second-longest charting album in the history of the Billboard Chart, surpassed only by Pink Floyd's *Dark Side of the Moon*. Despite the album's success, it has its critics who claim that these tracks are from Marley's Island years – he also has a massive back catalogue of other material to treasure. Others point out that it doesn't include his political or religious songs – the works that reveal the real man and the true legend.

SIDE A

UK CHART

01 IS THIS LOVE — NO. 9 IN 1978

02 NO WOMAN, NO CRY — NO. 8 IN 1981

03 COULD YOU BE LOVED — NO. 5 IN 1980

04 THREE LITTLE BIRDS — NO. 17 IN 1980

05 BUFFALO SOLDIER — NO. 4 IN 1983

06 GET UP, STAND UP

07 STIR IT UP

Singles for Bob Marley and the Wailers

Single that failed to chart

Hit for Johnny Nash

Hit for Eric Clapton

 7 Songs of freedom and defiance

 7 Songs of love and reassurance

MARLEY

80

BEST OF THE BEST OFS
(Sales in millions)

Artist	Sales
BOB MARLEY & THE WAILERS	28
MADONNA	30
ABBA	30
THE BEATLES	31
THE EAGLES	42

SIDE B

		UK CHART
01	ONE LOVE/ PEOPLE GET READY	NO. 5 IN 1984
02	I SHOT THE SHERIFF	NO. 27 IN 1977
03	WAITING IN VAIN	
04	REDEMPTION SONG	
05	SATISFY MY SOUL	
06	EXODUS	NO. 14 IN 1977
07	JAMMING	NO. 9 IN 1977

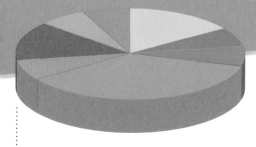

WHERE THE SONGS COME FROM

Album:
- KAYA
- NATTY DREAD
- UPRISING
- EXODUS
- CONFRONTATION
- BURNIN
- CATCH A FIRE
- UPRISING

LEGACY

79

MARLEY LIVES ON

All around the world reggae is synonymous with Bob Marley. His music and message inspire people from all races and backgrounds to dance, or to get up and stand up for their rights. People from locations as far flung as the shanty towns of South Africa and a remote part of the Grand Canyon in the US worship Bob Marley. One group of Native Americans called the Havasupai believe he is a prophet or god.

"I LIKE THE WORDS HERE. IT REMINDS ME OF THE PRAYERS OF THE OLD PEOPLE – THE WAY THEY USED TO PRAY. IT REACHES DOWN INTO THE SOUL – THE SPIRITUAL SOUL – WAY DOWN IN THERE."

—80-year-old member of the Havasupai people talking about 'Redemption Song'

The family business called the House of Marley produces sustainable music devices, including a turntable made from bamboo.

Rohan Marley runs a sustainable coffee business. "We, as the Marley family, won't be responsible for destroying the community. We want to bring life."

Marley's sons Damian, Stephen and Ziggy and grandson Bambaata Marley are recording music and spreading the Rastafari word.

MARLEY

Marley's child Cedella looked to her father for inspiration when she designed the Jamaican Olympic track and field team uniform in 2012.

The Rita Marley Foundation in Ghana is a charity supporting impoverished people around the world.

JAMAICA

Aston 'Family Man' Barrett still tours with the Wailers. Young Josh Barrett sings Marley's words, passing the Rastafarian message to the next generation.

In 2017, Marley was ranked 5th on the list of top-earning dead celebrities. At the time his estate was worth

$130 MILLION

Marley has

70

million followers on Facebook...

...and

4.2

million followers on Instagram

MUSICAL

One Love: The Bob Marley Musical by Kwame Kwei-Armah features 24 of Marley's original songs.

LEGACY

81

REGGAE HIT-STORY

1967 REGGAE GETS A NAME
'Do the Reggay' by Toots and the Maytals

1970 CLASSIC RASTA SOUND
'Rivers of Babylon' by The Melodians

197

1964 FIRST SKA HIT OUTSIDE JAMAICA
'My Boy Lollipop' by Little Millie

1969 FIRST INTERNATIONAL REGGAE HIT
'Israelites' by Desmond Dekker and the Aces

1972 FEATURE FILM REGGAE
Jimmy Cliff records the soundtrack to *The Harder They Come*

1990s REGGAE NEW-ZEALAND STYLE
Fat Freddy's Drop release *Based on a True Story*

2000 SONG OF THE MILLENNIUM
'One Love/People Get Ready' by Bob Marley and the Wailers is named the song of the century

2010 ONWARD

MARLEY

ART-
PPING
GGAE
an See
early
w' by
hnny
sh

1976

PETER GETS POLITICAL

'Legalise It' by Peter Tosh

1979 **REGGATTA DE BLANC**

The Police release *Reggatta de Blanc* or 'white reggae'

1980 **BRITISH TWO TONE**

Bands included The Specials, Madness, The Selecter, The Beat and Bad Manners

1974

ERIC SHOOTS THE SHERIFF

Eric Clapton covers 'I Shot the Sheriff'

1977

REGGAE AND PUNK UNITE

The Clash cover Junior Murvin's 'Police and Thieves'

1982

BOB MARLEY OF AFRICA

Alpha Blondy releases *Jah Glory*

1980s

REGGAE RE-INVENTS ITSELF

Reggae reinvents itself through Black Uhuru, Eddy Grant, Eek-a-Mouse and Yellowman

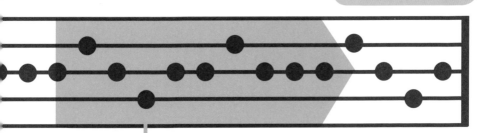

REGGAE RENAISSANCE

Young musicians and producers are re-inventing the reggae sound. Acts like Koffee, Cadenza, Protoje, Ady Suleiman, Chronixx, Major Lazer, the Skints, Lianne La Havas, Kiko Bun and Gentleman's Dub Club are seriously skanking. Meanwhile, mainstream artists like Ariana Grande and Ed Sheeran have been influenced by the reggae beat

The first reggae/ska hit outside Jamaica was Little Millie with 'My Boy Lollipop' in 1964. This young girl introduced the world to the infectious beat that had filled the dancefloors of Jamaica since the beginning of the 1960s. The love affair with reggae heated up in the 1970s, bringing hits for black and white artists hailing from all over the world. It has continued ever since.

LEGACY

BOB MARLEY

Jimmy Cliff and Bob Marley had a friendship going back to 1962 when they met in Kingston. Cliff produced the then 14-year-old Marley's debut tracks 'Judge Not', 'One Cup of Coffee' and 'Terror'. It was Cliff who first signed to Chris Blackwell's Island records and broke the international scene in 1972 when he starred in, and wrote music for, the film *The Harder They Come*. Success came later for Marley with the breakthrough album *Catch a Fire* (1972) and the 1974 album *Exodus*. Mammoth international sales soon established him as the new king of reggae, and an international cultural icon.

133 SINGLES

13 ALBUMS

GUITAR FACTS

Right-hander who played a Gibson Les Paul electric guitar or an acoustic guitar.

Inducted into Rock & Roll Hall of Fame

1994

ACTIVE 1962–81

11 CHILDREN

DIED 1981

BORN 1945

JIMMY CLIFF

ACTIVE
1962–
PRESENT

Inducted into Rock & Roll Hall of Fame

2010

4 GRAMMYS

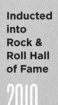

25 ALBUMS

262 SINGLES

GUITAR FACTS

Left-hander who plays a right-handed acoustic upside down but doesn't restring the guitar.

2 CHILDREN

LEGACY

85

TYPOGRAPHIC MARLEY

DREADLOCKS

KINGSTON

NESTA

NO WOMAN NO CRY

FREEDOM

KAYA

GANJA

THREE LITTLE BIRDS

JAMAICA

LOVE

RASTAFARIAN

BOB

HAILE SELASSIE

ISLAND RECORDS

UPRISING

ZIMBABWE

RUDE BOY

FISH TEA

ASSASSINATION ATTEMPT

REGGAE

1945

RELIGION

ONE LOVE

GUITAR

SURVIVAL

HOPE ROAD

CATCH A FIRE TRENCH TOWN THE WAILERS 1981 EXODUS MUSIC

FOOTBALL CANCER GIBSON JAMMING ADIDAS REDEMPTION NINE MILE MANGO OGO RITA EXILE

MARLEY LEGEND

CHILDREN NATTY DREAD AFRICA MUSIC SHOOTING MELANOMA

LONDON UNITED CONCERTS SMILE JAMAICA

TUFF GONG BUFFALO SOLDIER GHETTO PEACE ETHIOPIA

THE MARLEY MUSEUM

THE MARLEY MUSEUM

The museum at Marley's former home on Hope Road was curated by his wife Rita. This is the place to get a real Bob Marley experience as many of the rooms have been left as they were when he lived there and there is a life-size hologram of Marley performing in the One Love Peace Concert from 1978.

Bob's bedroom has a framed picture of Haile Selassie over the bed. His star-shaped guitar painted with birds and flowers is propped up against the bed.

There is an

80

seat movie theatre for showing Bob's concerts.

The

ONE LOVE

cafe serves up Bob's favourites like the kinky berry smoothie.

The TUFF GONG recording studio with original mixing board used by Marley.

56 HOPE ROAD KINGSTON

MARLEY'S HOME FROM 1975–1981

BECAME A MUSEUM IN 1986

Filled with Marley's gold and platinum discs, his Grammy Lifetime Award and the Order of Merit presented by the Jamaican government.

There are bullet marks in the walls where Marley survived an assassination attempt.

The shop

WAIL 'N SOUL

that Marley ran with Peter and Bunny in the 1970s has been recreated with the bicycle they used to deliver records.

TOO YOUNG TO DIE

The tragic irony at the heart of the many movements for peace and freedom in the twentieth century is the number of campaigners who suffered violent deaths for standing up for their beliefs. Marley escaped such a fate when an assassination attempt failed in 1976. Like his contemporary, John Lennon, he left behind a legacy of protest songs to help continue the fight for justice.

17 Kanaklata Barua
1942: Shot

18 Khudiram Bose
1908: Hanging

20 Andrew Goodman
1964: Shot

21 James Chaney
1964: Shot

23 Bhagat Singh
1931: Hanging

24 Michael Schwerner
1964: Shot

30 Steve Biko
1977: Died in police custody

35 Patrice Lumumba
1961: Execution by firing squad

36 Bob Marley
1981: Cancer

39 Martin Luther King
1968: Shot

39 Che Guevara
1967: Execution by firing squad

MARLEY

90

Age	Name	Year and cause
39	Malcolm X	1965: Shot
39	Dietrich Bonhoeffer	1945: Hanging
40	Emily Davison	1913: Suicide / trampled by horse
40	John Lennon	1980: Shot
42	Robert F. Kennedy	1968: Shot
42	Peter Tosh	1987: Shot
43	Victoria Mxenge	1985: Shot
46	John F. Kennedy	1963: Shot
49	Edith Cavell	1915: Execution by firing squad
50	Chris Hani	1993: Shot
62	Oscar Romero	1980: Shot

BIOGRAPHIES

**Judy Mowatt
(1952–)**
The Jamaican singer became part of the I Threes in 1974. In 1979, Judy released the highly acclaimed solo album *Black Woman* which she produced herself. Later, she became the first female reggae artist to be nominated for a Grammy.

**Rita Marley
(1946–)**
Born in Cuba, raised in Kingston, Rita met Marley in the mid-1960s through Peter Tosh. They married in 1966 and had three children together. After Marley's death she continued performing and spreading his message of love and defiance.

**'Bunny' Wailer
(1947–)**
Marley's childhood friend, born Neville O'Riley Livingston, was one of the original members of the Wailers. Bunny remained with the band until 1973 when he pursued a solo career, spent more time in Jamaica and devoted himself to Rastafarianism.

**Lee 'Scratch' Perry
(1936–)**
Jamaican dub mastermind and king of music production, Perry started his career at Studio One. In 1968, he formed his own label Upsetter Records. In 1973, he built his own studio, the Black Ark. Later, he recorded with The Clash and Beastie Boys.

**Ziggy Marley
(1968–)**
The eldest son of Bob and Rita Marley. At his father's request, he formed the Melody Makers with four of his brothers and sisters in 1979. Ziggy has played solo since 2003 and currently lives in Miami. He founded the charity URGE, which supports children in Jamaica and Ethiopia.

**Leslie Kong
(1933–71)**
The Chinese-Jamaican Leslie Kong was one of the first music producers to spot the talent of Bob Marley. Working from his restaurant and ice-cream parlour in Kingston, he launched the reggae and ska label Beverley's. Bob Marley and the Wailers returned to his studio in the late 1960s.

**Cedella Marley
(1967–)**
Cedella is the first child of Bob and Rita Marley. In 1979, she became part of the Melody Makers with siblings Ziggy, Stephen and Sharon. Currently, she is the CEO of Marley's recording label Tuff Gong International, runs 1Love and the marijuana brand Marley Natural.

**Chris Blackwell
(1937–)**
The British-born record producer formed Island Records in 1958. He released Little Millie's 'My Boy Lollipop' in 1964 which was the beginning of a roll that included reggae artists Toots and the Maytals and Bob Marley and the Wailers.

**Peter Tosh
(1944–87)**
Peter McIntosh met Marley in the early 1960s. After leaving the Wailers in 1974 he established himself as one of reggae's leading figures with his controversial solo album *Legalize It*. He was murdered in 1987 when gunmen entered his home.

**Coxsone Dodd
(1932–2004)**
The founder of Studio One, the first black-owned recording studio in Jamaica. Clement Seymour 'Sir Coxsone' Dodd is also credited with bringing ska and reggae to an international market.

**Marcia Griffiths
(1949–)**
In 1968, Marcia scored a solo hit in Jamaica with 'Feel Like Jumping'. In 1970, she sung with Marley on the reggae anthem 'Young, Gifted and Black' and she joined the I Threes in 1974. Her 1989 single 'Electric Boogie' became the top-selling single for a female reggae artist.

**Cindy Breakspeare
(1954–)**
Canadian-Jamaican jazz singer Cindy Breakspeare was crowned Miss World shortly before she began a relationship with Marley. They had one child, Damian, in 1978. They remained close friends and Marley helped her finance her shop 'Ital Craft' in Jamaica.

● family
● friend
● producer
● band member

INDEX

A
Adidas 22
African concerts 30–31
amps 63
Anderson, Al 72
assassinations
    attempt on Marley 26–27,
    66, 76
    of campaigners 90–91

B
Barrett, Aston 'Family Man'
    70, 81
Barrett, Carlton 70
Barrett, Josh 81
birth 14
Blackwell, Chris 27, 29, 41,
    60, 84, 93
Bob Marley Museum 41,
    88–89
Breakspeare, Cindy 19, 64,
    77, 93
Burnin' 58

C
calypso 44
Campbell, Naomi 29
cannabis 46–47
Catch a Fire 10, 40, 58,
    60–61, 71, 84
Chin, Vincent 'Randy' 40
Clapton, Eric 17
Clash, The 28, 83, 92
Cliff, Jimmy 20, 42, 60, 82,
    84–85
clothes 22–23
concerts 24–25, 30–31,
    32–33, 66–67

Confrontation 59
'Could You Be Loved' 68
Crocker, Frankie 68

D
death 32–34
Dekker, Desmond 20, 21
diet 54
Dodd, Clement 'Sir
    Coxsone' 20, 22, 40, 93
dreadlocks 50–51

E
Exodus 29, 59, 64–65,
    70, 84

F
family tree 18–19
football 28, 52–53
Ford, Vincent 'Tartar' 72

G
ganja 46–47
Garvey, Marcus 15, 48
'Get Up, Stand Up' 33
Gilbert, Tony 'Gilly' 54
Grant, Eddie 28, 53, 83
Griffiths, Marcia 70
guitars 62–63

H
Haile Selassie 29, 48, 88
hair 50–51
Hallyday, Johnny 43
Harry, Debbie 17
Havasupai people 80
Hendrix, Jimi 64
Higgs, Joe 20

hits
    of 1962 42–43
    reggae 82–83

I
'Is this Love' 29, 63

J
Jamaica 15, 16, 38–41
James, Marlon: *A Brief
    History of Seven Killings*
    76
'Judge Not' 20, 41, 42,
    71, 84

K
Kaya 29, 59, 70
Kingston 39, 40–41
Kinsey, Donald 27
Kong, Leslie 41, 92

L
Legend 8, 58, 78–79
Livingston, Bunny 20, 21,
    60, 70
London 28–29

M
McIntosh, Peter *see* Tosh,
    Peter
Malcolm, Cedella 14, 19, 20,
    21, 50
Malcolm, Omeriah 14
Manley, Michael 67
Marley, Bambaata 80
Marley, Cedella 18, 77, 81,
    93
Marley, Damian 19, 77, 80

MARLEY

Marley, David 'Ziggy' 18, 21, 77, 80, 92
Marley, Julian 19, 77
Marley, Ky-Mani 19, 77
Marley, Norval 14, 18, 21
Marley, Rita 20, 27, 29, 50, 51, 66, 70, 75, 76, 81, 92
Marley, Rohan 18, 77, 80
Marley, Sharon 18, 77
Marley, Stephen 18, 80
Marvin, Junior 9, 63, 68
Mayer, Roger 62, 64
Mayfield, Curtis 64
Melody Makers 77, 92, 93
mento 44
Morgan, Derrick 42
Morrison, Van 17
Mowatt, Judy 70

N
Nash, Johnny 24
Natty Dread 51, 59, 70
'No Woman No Cry' 72

O
Old Grey Whistle Test, The 23, 24
'One Cup of Coffee' 41, 76, 84
One Love: The Bob Marley Musical 81
'One Love' 8, 82
One Love Peace Festival 10, 67

P
Perry, Lee 'Scatch' 21, 40, 41, 92

Port Royal 39
'Punky Reggae Party' 28

R
Rastafarianism 20, 29, 30, 48–49
Rastaman Vibration 59, 70
'Redemption Song' 32, 63, 68
reggae
   hits 82–3
   roots of 44–45
Reid, Duke 41
ring 29, 34
rocksteady 45

S
Seaga, Edward 67
Seger, Bob 17
'Simmer Down' 20
Simon, Carly 17
ska 44, 45
Smile Jamaica 66
Songs of Freedom 58
Soul Rebels 58
Soul Revolution 58
Stewart, Rod 17
'Stir It Up' 23
studio albums 58–59
Survival 30, 59, 71

T
Taylor, Don 27
Toots and the Maytals 40, 41, 82
Tosh, Peter (Peter McIntosh) 20, 21, 60, 70, 77, 83, 93

Townshend, Pete 17
'Trench Town Rock' 8
Tuff Gong 40, 68

U
Uprising 32, 59, 68–69, 71

W
Wailer, Bunny 50, 70, 77, 92
Wailers 20, 70–71
Wailing Rudeboys 20, 40
Wailing Wailers, The 58, 71
world in 1945 16–17
Wossen, Crown Prince Asfa 29

Y
Young, Neil 17

Z
'Zimbabwe' 30